Shades
of
Grace

Building on Broken Pieces

By:
Khas Dock

GODZCHILD PUBLICATIONS

Published by Godzchild Publications
a division of Godzchild, Inc.
22 Halleck St., Newark, NJ 07104
www.godzchildproductions.net

Printed in the United States of America 2014—First Edition

Library of Congress Cataloging-in-Publications Data
Shades of Grace / Khasmin Dock

ISBN 978-1-937095-99-4

Table of Contents

Dedication

To the person that's a tear away from quitting.

To the soul that's too broken to move beyond the hurt.

To the mind asking the question,
"if God loves me, why is He allowing this?"

To the heart that's grown too hopeless to believe.

I penned this for you.

May the words on these pages meet you where you are.

Endorsements

When we are able to fully comprehend the measure of grace in our own lives, then and only then can we disseminate it to others." In this cutting edge- didactic book, *Shades of Grace*, Khas Dock transparently describes the measure of grace received in his own life. Through personal experiences and past hurts, he passionately reveals how grace has literally saved his life time and time again. Within this story of hope, redemption, forgiveness and healing, *Shades of Grace* is a manual that will change the course of this generation and the generations to come. When you are able to expose a past hurt that has been given the covering of grace, it no longer has a hold on your life. Dock profoundly releases the hidden treasure that we have been given through the grace of Jesus Christ. — **Paul Ellis, Author of** *When Saints Pray*

Shades of Grace is likened unto a spiritual chameleon. No matter where you are in your walk, the grace that the author Khas speaks of comes in just the right shade and color to match your issue. This message of grace is timeless and so heart gripping. Take the journey into this book and you will see how grace always shows up in different shades. — **Pastor Marquis Boone, Author of** *Til' the Last Drop*

There will be so many people that will be freed from reading *Shades of Grace*. The world will appreciate the leap that Khas has taken by exposing his truth, so that others may be freed. I anticipate the many testimonies that will come through this tool. — **Tasha Cobbs, Motown Gospel Recording Artist.**

Shades of Grace begins as an intimate view into the life of a young boy taken from his mother. Somewhere along the way, Khas eloquently creates a mirror with his words that shows you your own truth. His story is a reminder that pain does not discriminate and a testament that neither does Grace. — **Sarah Jakes, Author of Colliding with Destiny**

Shades of Grace paints a portrait of survival and triumph. This portrait offers hope to the little boy who is or was once a part of foster care, as well as, the "normal" person. *Shades of Grace* has many themes and takeaways throughout the story. One is the role of Khasmin evolving throughout his crisis at a young age, and coping with the challenge of adapting to change. Another imperative takeaway is the importance of acceptance. In certain situations, once they've become uncontrollable, we must be able to accept what's been done, cannot be undone; and therefore, acceptance is the first step in the healing process to change the situation from uncontrollable to controllable. Khasmin displayed his difficulties coping with change. He quickly learned you cannot fight change head on and expect to come out victorious. — **Malcolm Dock**

Courage. It takes a person of courage, topped with wisdom and humility, infused with strength, drenched in the Holy Spirit to write a book of this caliber. *Shades of Grace* open senses, and enable its readers to detect the hand of God over their lives—GRACE. — **Sheridan Davis**

Shades of Grace will bring many to the beginning of getting through some of the most difficult experiences that life brings, and it will begin to help initiate the healing process for those who have decided to live through what seems to be unbearable. The grace that God gives us daily can't ever be measured by the suffering that many of us endure, but may we continue to bless our God for His love that keeps us, and for the transparency that Khas has given us in Shades of Grace. — **Taneka Tuck**

Foreword

I don't remember when I met him; and I don't know how long I've known him. All I know is, I don't ever want to live life without him. He is the epitome of humility and my brother for life. His story is proof that God can turn the unfortunate and unpredictable tidal waves of life into peaceful waters and redemptive shores. Khas Dock is a gift to the world. He is not just a gift to Christianity or to Pentecostalism. His value cannot be fully encapsulated by a label or a designation. His heart is pure. His motives are genuine, and I applaud him for his boldness to open up the chapters of his heart for wounded soldiers like you and me to read.

After reading *Shades of Grace*, I was reminded again of the story of Peter in Luke 5. It is a familiar text that discusses Peter's failure at fishing, after having toiled all night to catch…nothing. Preachers tend to focus on how Peter should've remained persistent. He should've never left the scene. He shouldn't have been washing his net, they say, because that was a sign of surrender. Instead, Peter should've endured until the end.

But many times, what is preached on Sunday and what we live on Monday are diametrically opposed. It's just not realistic for Peter to fish and fish and fish and never get tired. The truth is, we all have had nights where we, like Peter, went fishing and caught nothing. We all have experienced the let down of high expectations when we set out to accomplish a task, in the name of Jesus, and we end up having to hide our failure beneath an edited status update or a fake "laid off" notice. All of us know what it's like to be Peter, but very few of us have been bold enough to, nevertheless, wash our nets.

You see, washing the net was not a sign of failure. It was a symbol of faith. By Peter washing his net, he was saying to his haters and to the naysayers "even though I didn't catch anything last night, I plan to get up and go fishing again tomorrow." A fisherman only washed nets if they intended to keep working. Most of us, after a bad episode of catching nothing, would've changed careers, but Peter exemplifies something eerily similar to the tenacity Khas has displayed in this book. Peter spent many nights waiting on these metaphorical fish to show up. Tears had been shed hoping that Jesus would come to the rescue and free him from the prison of his own realized failure, but just like Peter in Luke 5, Jesus doesn't show up to Khas Dock's house until Khas had given up on Khas's strength.

Isn't it funny how God always seems to come on the scene after you have told everyone 'the party is over!'"? Why is it that God conveniently waits until Larazus is stinking in order to come to Mary and Martha's house? Why would God wait for Abraham and Sarah to become old enough to envy everybody else's children, only to then give them the seed that would birth nations after their desired time of delivery. God's time table never seems to be in sync with ours... but now that I've read Khas's book, I'm so glad his ways are not like mine.

Khas's *Shades of Grace* is encouragement to Peter's like you and me. You will identify with so many parts of his life, but what I love most is that he meets you where you are without giving you impractical fluff that doesn't really fix the problem. Jesus shows up after Peter's failure, and I happen to believe that God strategically orchestrated every moment to the "T". How do I know? Because a crowd was following Jesus that day. They were hungry for a word from the Lord, but because there were no microphones during Jesus' day, he needed an empty boat to step into so that he could distance himself from the crowd, amplify his voice, and allow the people to hear him. Peter's failure was the empty boat Christ needed to preach his greatest sermon. Had Peter caught the fish, Christ may not have had a pulpit to preach from.

Makes me think that grace was the shade that kept Peter toiling all night. Makes me think that God held up Peter's quick fix so that others can have an eternal deposit. Makes me think that sometimes we don't get what we want not because we did something wrong, but because He can trust us with an empty boat. God loves to use our dark and empty moments as an opportunity to preach his greatest sermon. Khas proves it in his book, and through his life, and I'm sure…by the end of this journey, you will never see failure, loss, forgiveness, or grace the same.

To my little brother who has been an anchor of strength and encouragement to me during the most volatile and unpredictable times, I want you to know that I am so proud of you for allowing God to use your story for his glory. The crowd will be able to hear Christ more clearly because of your audacity to pen that which most only imagine. Readers, prepare for your life to be completely EN-GRACED!

— **Shaun Saunders**

Introduction

I had to be around 6 years old when those strangers showed up at my house. I had never seen them before a day in my life. Their conversation started to make me feel very strange and as time went by, I started to get more and more annoyed by their presence. I could not figure out the purpose of them being there or why they refused to leave and go about their business. I guess they were reading my mind because eventually they did leave. But they didn't leave alone. They left with something they didn't come with initially. In a car, with unknown strangers, my siblings and I were off to a destination unknown. That night our life hit a major turning point. As we traveled in the car headed to only God knows where, fear ran through my mind with a speed as fast as lightning. Riding down the street I remember seeing my mother. At that moment, my heart screamed the words I was too broken to utter: *"MOMMY, save me… save us."*.

From that moment onward, we began a journey none of us had planned to embark upon. Nobody had warned us about this journey. There was no GPS given so that we could find ourselves back at the place where we were involuntarily removed from. No one told us that such a journey even existed. Without any warnings or time to prepare, we were forced to embrace this journey and follow the many roads that it consisted of. We honestly didn't have much of a choice in the matter. The day my entire world transformed, is a day I will never forget. It was like standing outside, enjoying the sun rays of a beautiful summer day, and without any warning in the sky, the temperature drops, and the rain pours down profusely; and there I am standing there, cold and alone, wondering "where did the sun go?".

Just like an attic used for storage, I packed the memories of this day in black plastic garbage bags and shoved them in the attic—my mind—without any intentions of ever unpacking them. There was no part of me that ever wanted to revisit this episode of my life, so I changed the channel and prayed that I would never have to confront the facts; accept the pain; or recall this traumatizing event. I thought to myself, "Surely this is the method for guaranteed freedom". Little did I know, by avoiding acceptance, I wasn't escaping reality, I was imprisoning myself to the prison of my pain.

For years, I swam in a sea of suffering and affliction; and I couldn't comprehend why. I didn't know why God would sit on His throne, look down at me, but never motion to rescue me. Well, what was unbeknownst to me then, I now understand. God didn't rescue me, but He was my refuge. He didn't send a lifeguard because He was my Lifeguard; and on days I couldn't feel His nearness, His grace became my life-jacket. That's why I didn't drown. All along, He knew the testing was making my testimony and the pain was producing my purpose. He was breaking me in private so that He could send me to the public as a spokesperson of grace. Now, here I am, years later, to tell a story of how grace gives us the power to build from the broken pieces.

Chapter 1

Acceptance is Better Than Avoidance

fter all the crying, yelling, and carrying on had ceased, I had no choice but to come to terms with reality. It had become very clear to me that my life would not regress back to what I was accustomed to. Everything in me yearned to feel the embrace of my mother's love again. More than anything, I just wanted to be around her and my family again. Nothing else really mattered to me.

One day reality checked me and made me realize that the only thing left were the memories; and that burned me raw. Memories can be beautiful until you see that it is all they will ever be, and then, remembering becomes painful. Following that night, needless to say, things weren't easy for me, but I had to accept them. Things weren't easy for any of us. We were unwillingly introduced to DYFS (Division of Youth and Family Services) and the foster care system. From there, my worst nightmare began. I recall them assuring us that everything would be fine. But things weren't fine; things were as bad as they could possibly be. We were placed with a foster family while they searched for a willing and capable family member to temporarily place us with. After being bounced back and forth between different places, they eventually found a family member to send us with. I thank God for my cousin, Kirah, who stepped up to the plate and took us in. It was not the same as being at home with my mother, but it was surely a blessing to be with my own family. The English language doesn't have any words that can adequately express the level of gratitude I have for this act of love expressed by my cousin. Taking us in, while raising her only daughter alone, was more than kindness; it was a sacrifice. This gesture of love taught me a lesson I will never forget as long as I live. That lesson is: *pure love is identified by selfless sacrifice.*

After going through so much, I arrived at the conclusion that if nothing else is constant, change is. There aren't many things that are guaranteed to us in life, but change is undeniably one of them.

Things may change for the better or for the worst but you can be assured that things will change. Without your permission or approval, change will interrupt your life and introduce you to a new way of living. The manner in which you react to life's changes will ultimately decide how you, as a person, will be changed. Back then, I wasn't the best responder to things, especially not trials. Against my own volition, I eventually slipped into a dark pit. This pit was a place of confusion, pain, bitterness, resentment, anger, and hopelessness. I did not intend on landing into this position, but I was comfortable there because I knew exactly what to expect. As time progressed and my life continued to spiral out of control, I became immune to this place of agony and despair. This place had nothing to offer me and I was okay with that because as long as it had nothing to offer, I didn't have to fear anything being taken away from me. God knows, at this particular point of my life, I couldn't handle another loss.

Wherever escaping your reality leads to is a dangerous place. The reason it is dangerous is because upon your arrival there, you are welcomed with open arms by false immunity. By being immune to something, you have the ability to resist being affected by it. So, if you are falsely immune, what does that mean? It means that you don't actually have the power to resist it, you only have the ability to pretend that you are immune from it. Pretense is oftentimes the avenue that deters us from living out our purpose. Every moment lived in false immunity is another minute deducted from your destiny. The longer you stay there, the more of your true self you lose in the process.

I was so adamant about never experiencing pain again that I trained my mind not to respond to hurt. My response to pain was nonexistent because I had become so desensitized to reality. This false numbness lasted for a long while, but I eventually came to my senses and regained a desire to feel pain again. It sounds crazy, doesn't it? As crazy as it sounds, it was my reality. I literally began to feel as if I was living dead. I had deprived myself from feeling extremely too long and finally, I needed to feel what it was like to be human again; to hurt again; to merely feel again. So, I had to discover a new way to survive; and the only way I could do that was by accepting the broken pieces of my existence, and then building from there.

From experience, I can tell you that acceptance is so much better than avoidance. Avoidance has its perks but they are temporal and ultimately unbeneficial. Avoidance tells you that it is okay to not deal with the facts, but what avoidance doesn't tell you is that it has an expiration date. Avoidance is the friend that comes into your life, makes you feel like the bond will be everlasting, and then vanishes without reason or warning. One of the most potent and highly destructive tools in life is avoidance. It is a weapon that we form against ourselves, totally oblivious to the harm it causes to our spirit and our destiny.

As much as I didn't want to, and as much as I felt like I shouldn't have had to, accepting was the only way that my life could be positively redirected. It was the only way I could create a new normal. It was the only way to get to a point of wholeness. Creating a new normal demands work. The work that it takes to start over forces you to acknowledge that you cannot fix the malfunctioning components of your past; it forces you to understand that the only thing you can control is the present moment of your life. You have to understand that building a new normal is not about fixing, it is about recreating. It is about telling yourself, *"This is my chance to build something that is better than what broke me"*, and understanding that you have been endowed with the grace and strength to do it. Whenever you hit the reset button on life, you are given a fresh start. Before you can start over and build something new and something better, you have to expect that the work will take time and tears. Nothing about the healing process is easy or enjoyable. You are going to hurt in the process of healing;

YOU ARE GOING TO HURT IN THE PROCESS OF HEALING; BUT IF YOU WANT TO BE HEALED MORE THAN YOU ARE AFRAID OF HURTING, YOUR LIFE CAN BEGIN AGAIN AND YOUR HEART CAN LOVE AGAIN.

but if you want to be healed more than you are afraid of hurting, your life can begin again and your heart can love again.

Have you ever stopped to consider the rationality behind your refusal to accept all that has hurt you? What is the reason you choose to leave your pain unresolved? For some of us, our inability to deal with things was inherited from those in our family line. Mom and Aunty always swept their issues beneath the rug, denying the truth of things, and so you figure it is acceptable for you to do it, too. Being in an environment with people who have poor conflict resolution and problem solving skills, makes it easy for you to adopt the same behavior unknowingly. On the contrary, for others of us, we shun accepting things because we think it implies that we are agreeing with what hurt us. That is simply untrue. By deciding to acknowledge that something painful, unfair, and undeserving has happened to you does not mean you are validating the offense or the offender. Instead, it means, you recognize that if you don't accept the pain, the wound remains open and eventually begins to stain other areas of your life. Do away with the mindset that leads you to misunderstanding the purpose of acceptance and what it actually means.

Our personal rainy days are much like rainy days in real life. Before going to bed, have you ever planned your schedule for the next day? You strategically planned your wakeup time; you made your To-Do List and assigned a time of completion for each task; and you even picked out your attire for the day. You went to sleep determined and woke up motivated to accomplish what you planned, and then to your surprise, it is raining outside the next morning. What will you do now? Do you leave your To-Do List undone or do you put on your rain clothes and make things happen?

We don't have the ability to dictate the weather, but we certainly can choose to grab an umbrella and go about our day. When the weather and seasons change without forewarning, it can be disappointing, but life is still possible. Don't leave life un-lived because things didn't go according to your plans. Simply accept that it is raining, make adjustments, and live through the rain.

Grace Challenge

ACCEPT that it happened. ADMIT that it hurt you. ASK yourself what must be done for you to move on, and then do it.

Chapter 2

The Side Effects of Knowing

If you are anything like me, then you are the type of person who finds it extremely difficult to move on from a situation without knowing why things happened, and why they happened the way they did. As expected, my initial response to all that had transpired was, "Why?" I not only wanted to know why it happened but also why it happened to me. At this point, I was young and innocent; I didn't do anything to merit any of this. Pause. I feel like preaching right through here. Sound man, turn me up on the monitors! *Don't assume that everything that happens to you is a consequence of something that you have done wrong. Most of life's difficult moments are disguised preparation moments. You're not being punished; you're just being prepared. What you are enduring now, is empowering you for what's to come.*

Back to what I was originally saying before the preacher crept out of me. After experiencing such a painful separation, I needed to discover and understand the purpose behind everything. It was the only way the nonsense would make sense; and it was the only way I would be able to find peace. Due to how young I was when I was removed from home, I didn't know how to conduct my own research to figure out the "why" factor of things. I didn't know what questions to ask or who to direct the questions to. So, instead, I accepted the reasons that were given to me, by those who knew the details of the story better than I did. Almost every person had a different version of the story. My mom had one; DYFS officials had one; and my siblings had their own version as well. Again, I was young, so at the time I could not discern a lie from the truth. I simply believed what they told me. However, even though there were many inconsistencies in the stories being told, one thing remained consistent: drug abuse was a major reason behind the removal.

To learn that drugs destroyed the structure of my family, robbed me of my childhood, and altered my normality, made me distraught. Knowing this information made me extremely angry.

Bitterness and rage controlled my life on most days because I was so torn apart after learning the truth. How is one to cope knowing their whole life changed as the result of a drug addiction that didn't belong to them? It is extremely difficult finding a reason to smile after life has dealt you cards that should have been in someone else's hand. What would you do if you felt as if you were in a competition, and drugs won the love you desired and deserved? I wanted my family's love, but my wants were not enough to outweigh the stronghold of addiction. Could you find it in yourself to actually believe that you were more valuable than a quick fix? I sure couldn't. Is there anything worth smiling about, when your heart is broken at such a tender age? Absolutely not. At least, for me, it wasn't. My smile was replaced by a frown; and not the kind of frown that you have because someone stole your favorite toy. My frown told the story of a child with a broken heart, searching for helping hands to entrust the fragmented pieces of his heart to. So many questions flooded my thoughts and controlled my emotions. Not knowing what to do, I did what appeared to be feasible at the time. I suppressed the pain, hoping that one day it would altogether disappear. But it didn't. Instead, those suppressed feelings eventually emerged in the form of temper tantrums and displaced anger and hurt. I would get upset at the simplest of things. At times, I even gave unmerited treatment to people who did nothing but treat me well. For a very long time, I walked around angry at the world. I was what most would call a ticking time bomb waiting to explode. It was so easy for my buttons to be pressed and my mood to change all in the matter of seconds. I didn't want to be this way, but these were the side effects of knowing.

Knowing Doesn't Always Mean Closure

Does having all the details or enough details to get an understanding necessarily mean that you will get closure? In most situations, that is nothing close to what it really means. When you know all or enough information, curiosity usually forms, leaving you wanting to dig to find more information. One thing you should know about curiosity is: it has the potential to hurt you. Tame your curiosity, lest you go searching and find something you are unable to handle emotionally. Too many of us search for a truth we know that we are not ready to believe and questions we don't really want to know the answer to.

With all of the information I had, feelings of emptiness still remained. Knowing did not satisfy or settle me. There was nothing about knowing that filled the void I felt; neither did it answer the plethora of questions I had. Frankly, I still have questions today, which I would love to have answered; but because of the maturity I have acquired over time, I'm able to move forward without focusing on those unanswered questions. Yes, I want to know. But no, I refuse to give up on tomorrow because of what remains a mystery about yesterday. It took me some time, but I'm really okay with not knowing certain things—even the things that I feel I have a right to know. Honestly speaking, there are days that I wake up wanting to play detective, hoping that my findings would lead to me unknown details. But, I don't. You have to discipline yourself to become content with not knowing everything. When you do so, your mind and emotions are not shackled by undiscovered truths regarding your past. I'm at a place where I am confident that God will reveal things, in His timing if He deems it necessary.

If you are one to put your whole life on hold just to get clarity about things that happened years ago, consider stopping; you are doing yourself a major disservice. Why should you stop moving forward just to figure out things from back then? Your life right now is too precious to waste time and attention on what was. Let today be the last day that you rummage through the debris of your past

> ∽
>
> AT TIMES, YOU HAVE TO CHECK YOURSELF AND TELL YOURSELF: *I CANNOT GIVE ANOTHER SECOND TO BEING ANGRY; I DON'T HAVE ANY TEARS OF SADNESS LEFT TO CRY; I REFUSE TO LOSE ANOTHER NIGHT OF SLEEP OVER THIS. WHEN YOU LEARN TO COMMAND YOUR EMOTIONS, YOU GET A FIRMER GRIP ON CONTROLLING YOUR LIFE.*
>
> ∽

looking for details and answers. Stop searching before you become stagnant. You should value the progressiveness of your life so much that you are unwilling to be stagnated by what you don't know about your past. Never become so engrossed with knowing that you neglect growing. Don't be so hungry for details that you will put your whole life on hold to seek after them. If it is necessary for you to know, trust that God will make sure that information becomes available to you. Until He does, and even if He doesn't, simply take things for what they are and grow on. Not knowing won't kill you unless you allow it to. In fact, withheld information about past hurts is often times how God protects your heart from further breakage because He knows the fragility of your tender emotions.

The only thing knowing did for me, at the time, was make me mad. Can I be honest for a moment and share my truth? I wasn't just mad; I was mad as hell! As time went on, and I got older, I grew angrier because I just could not fathom the reality of things. The truth didn't just bother me, but it also broke me. As bad as I wanted closure, it just did not happen for me; or better yet, it didn't happen for me as quickly as I preferred. There were some more things I had to sort through; some people I needed to forgive; and some grudges I needed to release. If you are seeking closure, forgiveness has to happen first. The number one factor that stymies closure is the absence of forgiveness. Forgiveness is oftentimes blocked by stubbornness caused by deep rooted anger and hurt emotions. A stubborn person has a complexity about them that cripples their ability to get over anything because their anger prevents them from fully processing their pain. They are relentless and determined about remaining mad. Until the anger is properly dealt with, things won't get better. As a matter of fact, things are sure to get worse. Why? Because anger is much like cancer; the longer it's left unattended, the deadlier it becomes. If the cancer does not receive the treatment necessary in a timely fashion, the patient suffers severely and arrives at a higher chance of dying. In the same way, if you don't treat your anger soon enough, other areas of your life will suffer. It's better to forgive than to deal with the side effects of harboring grudges.

Please hear my heart on this. I am not saying that you

shouldn't ever be angry about unfortunate circumstances. It is your right to be. Nothing about anger is abnormal; all human beings experience it throughout their lifetime. However, it is not okay to remain angry. You have to discipline yourself to know when enough is just enough. At times, you have to check yourself and tell yourself: *I cannot give another second to being angry; I don't have any tears of sadness left to cry; I refuse to lose another night of sleep over this.* When you learn to command your emotions, you get a firmer grip on controlling your life.

The valuable time that you spend being angry, you can devote to taking the first step towards healing. Healing is a gift that you are deserving of. After you have forgiven, the peace that comes by letting go will instantly overwhelm you. Forgiveness frees you and it scars you. This scar replaces the wound (offense) that once governed your entire life. Embrace it. Own it. Love it. Most of us don't like looking at our scars because they remind us of the things we don't want to remember. However, I rather see the scars because when I look at them, I will find relief in knowing that what could have killed me, only bruised me.

You won't ever get healed until you let go of anger and any other emotion that is standing in the way of you forgiving. You won't stop being angry until you forgive what and who hurt you. Anger is a door that swings on the hinges of bitterness and isn't wide enough for closure to fit through. As difficult as it is, you must learn to forgive even the ugliest of pain. If you don't, there will never be a discontinuance of the pain; it will continue. Now is the perfect moment to ask yourself: how bad do I really want to stop hurting?

Forgiveness

There is no closure without forgiveness. A lot of us try to skip over forgiveness expecting to land at closure. If you really want closure, you must face forgiveness. There are no shortcuts or alternative routes. True forgiveness is the only road to closure. Take into consideration that I specifically wrote "true forgiveness". The reason I prefaced forgiveness with "true" is because, we attempt to get away with fake forgiveness. To put it more plainly: *if it's not authentic, it's not forgiveness.*

My first attempts at forgiveness were wrong. I didn't do it the right way; I did it my way. Truthfully speaking, although I didn't really want to forgive, I didn't really even know how to because I didn't know what forgiveness was. To me, forgiveness meant pushing things to the back of mind as if they had never happened. It took me a while to understand that forgiving involved letting go of the idea that the past should have happened differently. Forgiveness can do many things but one thing it can never do is make the present be what the past had potential to be. Forgiveness is about so much more than wishing the past, or the present, would change as a result of it. We must never forgive without an expectation to change what was or what is. We must forgive because we refuse to be weighed down by pain and offense. We must forgive for the sake of our future, our peace, and our emotional wellness.

In order to truly forgive, you have to actually accept what happened to you and mentally process the mixed emotions that resulted from the hurt you experienced. To forgive someone, without ever coming to terms with what they did to you, is not forgiveness at all. It's self-deception. Self-deception is convenient, but it isn't expedient for your emotional health and wellness. If you continue deceiving yourself, you will never be at peace with your past, and you will not know the freedom that comes with owning your own truth.

THE POWER TO LET GO COMES FROM WANTING TO. IF YOU WANT TO BAD ENOUGH, YOU WILL FIND THE STRENGTH TO ACTUALLY DO IT.

Forgive For You

I know just how it feels to want to withhold forgiveness. There are some things that break you so bad, the idea of ever being whole again seems impossible. But, that doesn't change that you have a responsibility to forgive. Surely, it is the last thing that you want to do, but it is what you have to do for the betterment of your life. As cliché as it sounds, the truth of the matter is: forgiveness is a gift from you to you even though you are giving it to them. When the gift box of forgiveness is open, the chains of offense are shattered, emotions begin to heal, and your heart finds hope to love and trust again. The moment that you forgive what happened to you, you sign a new lease on life, and enter a place of freedom and better living.

Our human nature has a way of making us believe that people deserve our resentment and bitterness because of the turmoil they have caused us. While that mindset is totally understandable, it is also unbeneficial and negative. There is no good that can come from thinking this way. The key to changing your mind about forgiveness is renewing your perception of it. Whenever your perception is molded by positivity, your outcome will be a positive one. Trust me, I did it and it works. If I found the strength to drop a load of bitterness, anger, and resentment that I carried for umpteen years, you can, too. The power to let go comes from wanting to. If you want to bad enough, you will find the strength to actually do it. You owe it to yourself and to your future to let it all go. Whatever your "*it*" is, I earnestly implore you to release it. After all, what good has holding on to it and not forgiving done for you? Ask yourself this question and then answer it truthfully.

Perhaps the reason you haven't had any peace is because you haven't yet forgiven. What if you haven't experienced happiness lately because you are carrying around multiple years of hurt with you? Maybe a new love hasn't found you because of the old pain that still controls you. As long as old baggage fills your life, there will be no room for anything new to enter. When you choose not to forgive, you are signing a contract that warrants stagnation and stunted growth.

Do It For Real

If you are going to forgive, do it for yourself; but more importantly, *do it for real.* There is no personal advantage associated with rendering false forgiveness. It has proven to do more harm than good. Genuine forgiveness is the better route to take. After many arguments and many years, I came to understand this. There was a point when I habitually brought up what my momma did anytime that we would argue. We could be going at it about something as simple as me going into her snack stash; and the moment she said something I didn't like, I would bring "*that*" up. I would use every opportunity to remind her of how she hurt me. I would always dig up things that I claimed to have buried and left in the past. Yeah, it was that bad. Eventually, reality checked me and I became aware that I didn't really forgive my mother; I merely just pretended to be over what happened.

Some of you reading this are in the very place I was once. You claim to have forgiven that person, but you are always throwing what they did to you back in their face. With each opportunity that presents itself for you to take them down Memory Lane, you do so eagerly. That's not how it goes. True forgiveness is an expression of true love; and true love never keeps a record of wrongdoing. I'm not saying this to imply that you are required to forget what happened to you. That would be an unfair and unreasonable demand to place on anyone. However, I am saying that you should be better at not revisiting the offense each time you are upset. The overall purpose of forgiveness is to propel you forward, not backwards. Forgiveness has only one direction, and that is forward. It is the bridge that transports you from Offense to Freedom.

Forgiveness Isn't A Fix for the Past

Forgiveness cannot be effective if you don't have an understanding of its purpose. When you don't know the function of something, using it for all the wrong reasons is both common and inevitable. We tend to treat forgiveness as a restoration agent to fix the *past*, when in fact, it was never meant to be that. You must understand one thing: *forgiveness is not a janitor whose job is to clean up the mess made in the past.* Forgiveness pens peace on the pages of your present and ensures that the future chapters of your life are free of bitterness from prior pain. Until you see it as such, you will continue trying to fix what is broken instead of creating new memories and building fresh relationships. The reality of forgiveness is: every "I forgive you" will not reopen the book, just like every "I'm sorry" won't make a person who doesn't want to be in your life stick around.

Allow me to tackle this from a more personal standpoint, pinpointing my relationship with my father. For more than twenty years, my dad was not around. I knew of him but I didn't know him. The only bond we shared was biological. For those of you who are familiar with the side effects of having an absentee father, you understand the highs and lows of the roller coaster fatherless children ride the majority of their lives. At one point, the only thing I knew about my dad was his name and the alleged reasons for him not being around. There were no memorable moments that we shared for me to reflect on; so in essence, I did not have much to miss. How can I miss someone I never knew? How do you cry over a bond that was never built? He did not teach me how to ride my first bike; nor did he take me to the barbershop on Saturday morning to get my hair cut. I'm a total stranger to the affectionate bond shared between a dad and a son. It goes without saying how unfulfilled that made me feel for years.

...FORGIVENESS IS NOT A JANITOR WHOSE JOB IS TO CLEAN UP THE MESS MADE IN THE PAST. FORGIVENESS PENS PEACE ON THE PAGES OF YOUR PRESENT AND ENSURES THAT THE FUTURE CHAPTERS OF YOUR LIFE ARE FREE OF BITTERNESS FROM PRIOR PAIN.

It wasn't long ago that my dad came back into the picture. When I received the first letter from him while he was incarcerated, I was unsure how to feel. A part of me wanted to shred the letter without ever opening it; another part of me wanted to cry tears of joy because reunification seemed promising. I had so many mixed emotions, and to be honest, I still do. I could have easily decided not to communicate with him as a means of repayment for not being present. It was definitely a thought, but I had to remind myself that I didn't have that right. Making people pay for their mistakes is a right that belongs to God only. He is the only one with the authority to seek vengeance.

It doesn't matter how deeply you have been cut, you don't have the right to strike back. God will handle those who hurt us and He will do it when and how He wants to; and it will likely be done in private. Don't ever assume that because you didn't personally witness the chastisement it didn't happen.

Despite how difficult it was, I forgave my dad. Actually, long before he ever returned to my life, I had forgiven him. I did so because it was needed for my *now* not because I wanted to make up for what happened *then*. I would be a liar if I said that I don't wish we could go back and make up for lost time. What son doesn't yearn to be fathered? What child doesn't want to one day look back and reflect on the precious moments spent with their father? I'm no different than other sons who want to have at least one laughable story to share with their kids about their old man; but I don't, and I have grown to accept that. Time has taught me to be okay with the things I can't change or control. What I do have, however, is the story of how he didn't remain gone. He could have certainly made the decision to remain out of my life, but regardless of the years that had gone by, he sought after me. For that, I have no choice but to respect and honor him. Although he can never right his wrongs, he is at least making the effort to create a better right now.

In all of this, I learned some powerful lessons:
1. There will be times when someone you forgave for hurting you returns to your life. Your response to their return will prove how sincere your forgiveness was.
2. At the heart of forgiveness should be an intentional decision to change your position from HURT to HEALED. Before your position can change, your mind has to change and accept that forgiveness isn't a license to go back and reconstruct the past.
3. Having an "it is what it is" mentality will save your sanity. You will drive yourself crazy trying to change what you don't have the power to control.
4. Whether being given to someone else or to yourself, forgiveness is grace in action. It is one of the deepest ways to love yourself and others.

5. Don't let your decision to forgive depend on their apology. Even if they never tell you that they are sorry, forgive them anyway. The apologies you deserve the most are typically the ones you will never get. The good news is, you can survive without an apology. Grow on.

Grace Challenge

If you are struggling with forgiveness, ask God for the grace to make forgiving easy. He will give it to you. If you are simply choosing not to forgive because you feel like you shouldn't have to, you should consider the times you have been forgiven by God and others. The grace you are withholding from them is the same grace God gives you despite how undeserving you are.

In times when forgiveness becomes difficult, contemplate these two passages:

∽ Colossians 3:13 (NIV) Bear with each other and forgive one another if any of you has a grievance against someone. Forgive as the Lord forgave you.

∽ Matthew 6:14 (NIV) For if you forgive other people when they sin against you, your heavenly Father will also forgive you.

Chapter 3

Faith Issues

Hearing someone speak about their trust issues isn't anything out of the ordinary these days. Without much searching, you can surely find a multiplicity of people who will admit to having problems in the area of trusting. Some will attribute their trust issues to their experiences in dating and others will attribute theirs to many other reasons. Regardless of what the reason may be, the point is, everyone will be met with the challenge of trusting. But that isn't what this chapter is about. I want to address a problem that is somewhat similar to trust issues—*faith issues.*

Considering all that you have read about my life up until this point, saying that I struggled with my faith should come as no surprise to you. With all that I have dealt with, I often found myself in a position where I was too pressured to operate or respond in faith. No matter how hard I tried, some days I just couldn't seem to find a thread of hope to cling to. And even though I wanted to believe that my days would get brighter, I couldn't ignore the dark days that I was living in. I prayed for the best but after I said "Amen", and came out of prayer to go about my day, bad was there waiting on me. Living by faith and not by sight becomes a difficult task when everything you are seeing looks nothing like what you have been promised. God made a promise that He would perfect everything concerning me, but that promise became harder to believe each second that things remained the same instead of changing.

Faith issues have outstanding mannerisms; they don't ever show up unannounced. In fact, they come by invitation only. The million dollar question is: who sends the invitation to them? They receive an invitation from doubt. If you want to know the origin of your faith issues, find out where your hope stopped and doubt began. As soon as hope is subtracted from the equation, your faith and belief is divided. The moment when I stopped trusting that things would work for my good, is the very moment that my hope started to dissipate. There is no possible way for faith and unbelief to operate in the same place. Control your feelings so that you never become unsure about God's plans of prospering you (Jeremiah 29:11 KJV). The more our feelings are controlled, the less faith issues we will have to deal with.

Faith That Conquers Anything

If you have been in church for a decent amount of time, you have more than likely heard the song, "Faith That Conquers" at least once. It was probably an every Sunday song at your church at one point in time. The song makes a declaration about having strong faith---a type of faith that can conquer anything. We sing this song with much passion but do we really believe what we are singing? Do we truly believe that there is such a faith that can overcome anything? Better yet, do we even possess this faith that we sing about? I will be the first to answer by saying: not all of the time. To be truthful, if I had to sing this song on many occasions, it would have gone something like this: "I have the faith to conquer some things."

There are two things about undergoing a process of suffering that cannot be disputed: *suffering will test your faith; and it will not only change the* **content** *of your prayer, but it will change the* **way** *that you approach prayer.* Allow me to share with you how I know this to be true. As stated earlier, my removal from home was in relation to the use of drugs. Well, this drug issue went far beyond this one event. In fact, drug addiction was something that has plagued my family for years, and still does. By witnessing the detrimental effects drugs and alcohol have had on my family, it hurts my heart. Very often, the pain I felt pushed me into prayer. I didn't just go into prayer, crying out "God fix it!" I approached prayer with a purpose: *total deliverance and freedom from drug/alcohol addiction.* Therefore, the content of my prayer had to match the purpose behind the prayer. Everything inside of me trusted that God would do it. I had faith because I knew God had power. But faith began to disappear when I noticed there was no change in their condition after spending so much time praying. How could I continue believing when it appeared that God wasn't moving? Faith issues.

How You Wait Matters

Psalm 27:14 (KJV) Wait on the LORD: be of good courage, and he shall strengthen thine heart: wait, I say, on the LORD.

Obviously, the more that you pray is the more that you will expect. Your prayer closet is the birthing place of your expectations. It is the place where anticipation is conceived. At some point, we all expect our private prayer life to transform the reality of our public life. No one prays for healing and expects to remain sick. Neither does anyone ask for a spouse and expect to continue living their life as a single person. This is why we eagerly await a breakthrough after we have sought the Lord in prayer. Although we would like to witness an instantaneous turnaround after we seal our prayer with an "Amen", the truth is, we must wait. We must not only wait but we must wait on the Lord.

The way in which you wait matters. As a point of fact, it is the difference between enduring and failing your waiting period. Waiting on the Lord teaches you patience and strengthens your heart. If your heart is ever weak while waiting, it is because you haven't been waiting on the Lord, you have just been waiting for things to change. The Bible ensures us that, "they that wait on the Lord, shall be renewed in their strength..."(Isaiah 40:31 KJV). Whenever you wait on the Lord, He will sustain you, keep your mind in perfect peace, and give you the grace to go forward instead of becoming stagnant. So, if you want to survive your waiting period, change the way that you wait. Don't ever confuse waiting for results to be the same as waiting on the Lord. There is a difference between the two. If you arrive at the end of your waiting period without the results you wanted and your faith does not fail, that is proof that you were

GRACE IS THE SUPERNATURAL GUIDANCE THAT HOLDS YOU TOGETHER AS YOU TRAVEL TO GLORY; THE PLACE WHERE YOUR REWARD IS.

waiting on the Lord and not just waiting on results.

My biggest failure with waiting was I refused to be patient. Scratch that. I did not even give patience a fair chance because all I wanted to see when I came out of prayer was a quick turnaround; but I eventually learned that waiting is a process that produces maturity and endurance. When you make a real decision to wait on the Lord, you get to a place where you expect your character to be perfected more than anything. These are the lessons that waiting on the Lord teaches. How do you wait on the Lord? You worship Him; you spend time with Him, not asking for things but simply enjoying the beauty of His glory. Learn how to enjoy the process of being perfected in God's presence as you wait. If you do this, you will be okay with living without what you are praying for.

Don't lose your worship in the wait. Most of the time, so many of us are so concerned about what we are waiting for, we direct all of our focus on that thing without even noticing that our worship lifestyle is slowly fading. If what you are waiting on puts you in a place where you don't spend any time, or enough time, with God, why would God grant it to you? Don't ever expect God to release something that will potentially strain your relationship with Him. He won't do it. Maybe God has you waiting not because you aren't ready, but because your affection and attention is in the wrong place. Is your desire for "that" outweighing your desire for God?

Keep Your Faith Guarded and Grounded

Waiting on a manifestation requires mature faith. Mature faith is when what you see doesn't alter what you know. In other words, regardless of what your present reality is, you know that is not the final picture. Mature faith produces a determination that helps you to never allow the facts to confuse your faith. Although it appears that the manifestation may never show up, please trust that it will. It hasn't arrived yet but that doesn't mean it isn't on the way. My tears were not in vain and neither are yours. Don't let your faith fail while you are waiting. Don't let this brokenness steal your belief in God's power. Don't tap out of the fight. Don't settle for the current state of your situation. Your present suffering is producing your future glory. Certainly, I know it's hard accepting that your public life contradicts your private prayers. Contrary winds are blowing all throughout your life; and the harder they blow, the more scattered your faith becomes. You are hurting because in your prayer time, you earnestly pray that your mother is freed from drug use but every time you see her, she is still strung out. You have been praying for the presence of your absentee father, but he is still gone; and it kills you every single day. You have spent innumerable years asking God to save your son from the streets; but he is getting deeper involved in street activity, and your days are spent fearing that he will be incarcerated or killed. And yes, I know you are right at the brink of signing those divorce papers because your marriage is still drifting downhill, even though you have been praying, fasting, and believing for it to be salvaged.

You need to be reminded that your story does not end here. This pain is just another page in your book of life. I consider that your present sufferings are not worth comparing with the glory that will be revealed in your life. (Romans 8:18 NIV). In between glory and suffering is a survival tool called grace. Grace is the supernatural guidance that holds you together as you travel to glory; the place where your reward is. Grace is the reason why your faith has not failed completely. Cling to the little bit of faith that you have remaining and use it to keep going.

Grace Challenge

Faith can only be as strong as the person to whom it belongs. Feed your faith with positive thinking and the substance that is God's word.

Chapter 4

Development not Definement

Trrue liberty occurs when you come to realize that what you go through does not define who you are. Everything that you have gone through, are going through, and will go through has one purpose: **to develop your character and shape your life's purpose.** Afflictions, trials, tribulations, hardships, downhill experiences, calamity, separation, seasons of isolation, pain, and turmoil- are all used to shape and strengthen you for a greater purpose in life. Most times, you will never understand why you were in the furnace of affliction, until the flames die down and the smoke has cleared. This is why it is so crucially important to never give up whenever you are encountering the storms of life. If you quit during your suffering, you won't see the significance of your pain.

In Psalm 119:71 (NIV), David pens, *"It was good for me to be afflicted so that I might learn Your decrees."* This verse contains such a deep level of meaning in a number of ways. At first, my initial response to this verse was, "How is affliction good?" For the life of me, I couldn't find the sense in this; but thank God for revelation. I understand this scripture more now than when I first read it. God has a way of unveiling the meaning of scriptures at the appropriate time. And when He does, that is when we realize the connection between His Word and our circumstances. That is the beauty of God's Word.

If I had to interpret what David was saying, I could draw up many conclusions from this verse. One thing is unquestionable, and that is, David realized that his times of afflictions were moments of growth. They were also opportunities for him to experience God's grace and delivering power in a new way. Two things stick out in this scripture. The first is, David says: "It was good for me that I was afflicted" Take into consideration that David did not say "It is good for me that I am being afflicted" What point am I attempting to make here? David did not originally believe that afflictions were good. Hence, his use of the word "was". There's a lesson in this: it's not until you have endured affliction that you will appreciate experiencing it. No one appreciates being broken until after they have survived the pain and realized how much better they are because of it. The second thing that sticks out in this scripture is he proceeds to say, *"... **so that I might learn your decrees"**.* In other words, affliction teaches you the depths of God. From a personal standpoint, I know that if it had not been for all of the downs in my life, I wouldn't know God the way that I do today. Without affliction, I wouldn't value the importance of prayer. Without ever experiencing trials, I wouldn't have discovered the power in worship. That's basically what David was saying here.

The second you come to this exact realization, your perception of life will be positively altered forever. If you can change your perception of affliction, so that you are able to identify the good in it, it will change your life for the better. Too frequently we make the mistake of seeing things that are designed to bless us as being a curse. We do this because we have a twisted perception and concept of life and the purpose of life's circumstances. We also do this because we fail to consider that God has vowed to deliver us from each of our afflictions. There will never be an instance where you will find yourself dealing with life on your own. In fact, Psalm 34:18 (NIV) tells us that God is close to the brokenhearted and saves those that are crushed in spirit. You will deal with difficult times and you will even experience plenty weak moments as you journey through life; it's guaranteed, but so is God's grace. Wherever you are in life, grace is there with you. Grace is there to help you when you are too weak to help yourself.

Give God His Job Back
The issue most of us have is, we don't know how to submit to suffering; so our inability to submit causes us to box God in. As a consequence, we attempt to deliver ourselves from situations. Delivering ourselves is not listed in our job description. We have been employed to suffer in faith, while remaining confident that our Employer has the sovereign responsibility of delivering us. Brother David puts it this way: *"Many are the afflictions of the righteous: but the*

Lord delivereth him out of them all," Psalm 34:19 (KJV). David had an understanding that God didn't need any assistance with doing His job, so he committed himself to being a diligent sufferer and trusted God to compensate him with deliverance. Today, you ought to challenge yourself to do the very same thing. Give God back His job by taking your hands completely out of the situation. Whatever your plight is, know that it is best handled in the hands of God. He shall deliver you, but He cannot do it if you are preoccupied with trying to do it on your own.

For too long, I wasted precious time trying to fix what was broken, unaware that I was causing more damage and holding up my own deliverance. Similarly, some of you reading this have been doing the same thing. Learn to trust God with the broken pieces of your life. He is the only one that can make a masterpiece out of the mess. As you cope with trying times, understand that things have to be exactly what they are so that you will become exactly who God intends for you to be. None of what you have dealt with, or ever will deal with, will be by happenstance. God has a divine plan which has been custom made to perfectly fit your life. In this plan, He has scheduled sporadic intervals of pain for the intention of positioning you for great works. The pain might be uncomfortable, but it is necessary. Every low place in life prepares you for a high place. Every tear that you shed waters the harvest that awaits you on the other side of suffering.

> *WE HAVE BEEN EMPLOYED TO SUFFER IN FAITH, WHILE REMAINING CONFIDENT THAT OUR EMPLOYER HAS THE SOVEREIGN RESPONSIBILITY OF DELIVERING US.*

Pursue the Purpose

The pain inflicted by God will always have justifiable reasoning. It isn't God's character to cause pain without allowing something new to be born *(Isaiah 66:9 KJV)*. Some of your greatest assignments will be birthed through periods of affliction. As you walk through difficult times in life, keep your minds and eyes open so that you won't miss the instructions for what to do once the difficulty has ceased. These instructions will often come through dreams, visions, ideas, and the like.

What if the whole point of your homelessness was just for you to open a shelter, to provide refuge and resources to people who are where you once were? Maybe you survived that abusive relationship so that you can become an advocate against domestic violence and mentor those who have been affected by it. Perhaps this period of unemployment is simply an open door for you to activate that business plan that you have pushed to the side for so many years; that plan that will bring improvement to your church and community, and your life. There is a reason behind it all. Underneath our pain is the roadmap to our purpose; you simply have to search through the tears to discover it. Searching won't be easy but it is worth the effort. Even if you get lost while looking, you can't stop until you locate the treasure. You suffered too long not to get something out of it. You suffered for too long for your destiny not to begin where the suffering ends.

We spend too much time complaining about what we are going through, but not enough time trying to figure out what the exit plan is once we are delievered. The reason you are going through is because there is something that God wants you to do once you come out. After being delivered from my childhood anguish, I found myself attracted to broken people. For so long, I didn't understand this unusual attraction, but now I do. This attraction existed because God was prompting me to be an encourager and an intercessor for people who battle with brokenness.. Now, I have become the person who prays for others instead of judging and cares when others aren't the least bit concerned. I want the way I live to be why someone finds a reason to hope again. Every day, *"Lord, keep me sensitive to those around me"* is my humble prayer because I never want to miss an opportunity to love on a broken hearted person. Sometimes all a person really needs is enough compassion to show them they aren't alone. For me, a part of my purpose is being hope to the despondent. Your purpose might be something different, but you have to discover it while you are being developed, so that when you are finally delivered you can begin to fulfil that purpose.

Each step of life won't lead to a good place, but wherever you end up will be a place with an opportunity to grow. Growth is a process of development intended to prepare you to be efficient for where you are growing to. While growing, expect for all aspects of your life to be stretched. Your character will undergo severe pressure, but just like diamonds must endure pressure before being put on display, the same is expected of us. Bring your perception to a level where you are able to embrace the idea that hardships develop you and not define you. If you grow through this, when you get there, you won't be lacking in anything. The best part of it all is, as you are growing from one place to the next, grace is there every step of the way. Grace comforts you when the growing pains make you uneasy; and places momentum behind you when you are feeling too weak to stay on course. Keep your focus on the bigger picture and find motivation in knowing: ***affliction molds you into a person strong enough to fulfil the assignment on the other side of your suffering.***

Grace Challenge

Make this your affirmation: *"There is something better waiting at the end of this"*. It is all about what you say. Words matter most in times of trial. Most of us haven't seen the promise associated with our pain because of the many negative words we speak while we are hurting. Season your words with positivity. Negative speech will only prolong your process.

Chapter 5

Matters of the Heart

When your only source of security is no longer existent, where does that leave you emotionally? With each heartbeat, you feel unwanted. In the company of people, you fear that your smile is not big enough to cover your insecurities. You feel less confident than before. You feel rejected and abandoned. An "everybody is out to get me" mentality develops, and you begin to feel susceptible to being taken advantage of. From these formidable feelings, it is easy for a wall built with bricks of reticence and reluctance to form. You use this wall as a defense mechanism to keep suffering and disappointment from gaining access to your life and your heart. Go ahead, ask me how I know. This was me at one stage; but considering my story, could you really blame me? When I was separated from my mom and siblings, I was a child. Consequently, the only security that I had known, came from home. When you are a child, there is not much that you worry yourself with because your main source of provision and protection comes from your parents and your household. Given this truth, when I was removed, my security was removed as well. As a result, I spent most of my childhood and early teenage years not knowing who to trust, or even how to trust if I wanted to. It wasn't until my late teenage years, right before becoming an adult that I started to develop relationships of any kind. Prior to then, I really didn't care to get to know anyone; I felt like everyone who came around wouldn't stay around. After too many goodbyes, you become afraid of hellos because no matter how sweet they are, a part of you doubts that they will last. These feelings, however, didn't outweigh my desire of wanting true relationship with people. I was scared, but I was willing to take the risk. At the end of the day, I wanted to experience the beauty of having genuine connections, so I pursued them.

As humans, we are innately wired with the need for companionship. In some way, every human desires friendship and to have a sense of belonging among their peers. Wanting to belong is not a problem; the problem presents itself when wanting to belong turns into a need to belong. There is a thin line between the two. Sadly, many of us are not successful at making this distinction. When you only want to belong, you are absolutely okay if you end up not belonging. On the other hand, when you feel that you need to belong, you find it hard to function outside of friendship, and therefore, you will attempt to walk on water just to feel like your presence in someone's life is wanted and meaningful.

Anytime you have to go out of your way to prove yourself to someone, your value is already nonexistent to them. Whenever your presence in someone's life means something to them, they will show you with their actions. Actions will prove the level of a person's appreciation for you. You should never have to play the Guessing Game to figure out where you stand with anyone. An authentic friendship doesn't leave space for uncertainty because when it is real, it is solidified. It took me quite a while to learn this lesson. Had I known this earlier on, I would have never given my best in bad relationships. But, that is the consequence of feeling the need to belong. Too often, I found myself being loyal to people who did not understand loyalty's worth or significance. The commitment and support I deposited into some connections went unappreciated and unreturned. It had nothing to do with me not being a good enough friend because I've always been that; but it had everything to do with me casting my pearls before swine. You can give until you go broke but unless you are investing in good stock, you will never get a return. As hard as it might be, let wisdom fuel every investment that you make. There is a high probability that wisdom will defy your logic and your feelings but it will never steer you wrong. Wisdom looks out for you when you are too naive to look out for yourself.

While we are on the topic of investments, I have to say this. When it comes to our friendships, romantic relationships, careers, ministry responsibilities, and the like, we are the best investors. It does not matter what it takes or costs, we will give it without hesitation. Sacrificing, for the majority of us, is the way we say thanks; it is the way that we prove our love and loyalty. However, when it comes to ourselves, we usually have nothing left to give. A lot of times we allow our needs to go unmet and our problems to go unresolved because we have put ourselves last while others hold first place in our lives. There is nothing wrong with loving those you are in connection with but don't allow yourself to become a slave to loyalty.

Learn how to make deposits into your own life. If you are always giving, what are you saving for yourself? If you are a giver by nature, it is understandably a challenge for you to pull completely away from supporting and giving to others. That isn't what I am asking you to do, but I am cautioning you to be a better investor. Apply discipline to your giving so *Insufficient Funds* won't be the error message that you receive when you try to make withdrawals for yourself. In other words, give to yourself and be okay with others giving to you as well. It is our giving nature that usually robs us from receiving. Whenever you don't leave room for people to give back to you, you inadvertently turn those individuals into people of entitlement. Having a sense of entitlement tells a person they have a right to everything but a responsibility to give nothing in return. This is how one-sided relationships are created. Anyone that feels entitled to you will take advantage of you instead of appreciating you.

> *APPLY DISCIPLINE TO YOUR GIVING SO "INSUFFICIENT FUNDS" WON'T BE THE ERROR MESSAGE THAT YOU RECEIVE WHEN YOU TRY TO MAKE WITHDRAWALS FOR YOURSELF.*

Build the Right Way

Okay, let's get back to what this chapter is about—matters of the heart. An insecure person has a need for validation. It is the silent cry of every insecure person's heart to feel attached to someone or something that makes them feel important and wanted. On a consistent basis, they need to hear how amazing they are; they need to be reassured of how much they matter; they simply need affirmation and affection. Without it, there is no chance of them being totally secure within themselves.

A person dealing with insecurity issues is not necessarily someone who has self-esteem issues. Personally, I can attest to that because my insecurity didn't have anything to do with an identity crisis; it had everything to do with trying to love from a broken heart. Whenever your heart is bruised, you are not in a position where you can properly love someone. A broken heart is a heart that is in need of repair. My issue was, instead of attacking my insecurity, I let it linger. I allowed it to make me settle for the friendships I knew I was too good for. Why? An insecure person yearns for security, so they will settle for what is available even if it isn't right for them.

When you build relationships with a whole heart, you operate in wisdom. You don't hit accept on every friend request. You wait things out. You look for warning signs. You make sure there is potential even if it is accompanied by flaws. But when you try to build from an insecure heart, you tend not to use wisdom or good judgment. Those that know me, know my fondness when it comes down to friendship and commitment. I believe in loyalty. I live loyalty to the best of my ability; and although there have been times when I have missed the mark, and I did things contrary to true loyalty, I never lost my willingness to become better at it. I have always prided myself in being what I want to see in others. It is unfair to demand anything that you don't demonstrate. If you want respect, give it. If you want honesty, tell the truth. If you desire trust, be trustworthy. The standards that we expect others to meet must be the same standards that govern our lives. If not, we are nothing more than hypocrites searching for everything without giving anything. Truthfully, we all want something real; something that will last; something that we can build and be proud of.

Loyalty, for me, is a source of security and reassurance. When I give my commitment to someone, I do so with intentions on proving that I appreciate their presence in my life. When I give my commitment to something, I do so with intentions to prove that I recognize its purpose. But for some reason, no matter how much I gave or how hard I tried, I seemed to constantly come up short. The areas I made investments in, I was lacking in within myself. For some time, I was confused but then a light came on and illuminated the incomplete areas of my life. Since that moment, I have been doing the work to fix my life. *Iyanla, I'm sorry for not hiring you for the job.* Now, I give my loyalty, dedication, and devoutness because I want to, not because I need it in return for validation.

For the person who is struggling with matters of their own heart, I want to offer a simple suggestion: *build outside relationships when you know that you are whole enough on the inside.* We must be very careful of the bonds we build. If the bond is not created on the right foundation, what good does committing to it serve? The key to forming healthy relationships is building them on sturdy foundations. The strength of what your relationships are built on ultimately determines what will come of those relationships. If you want it to last, build it properly. A lot of people build on a lie and expect longevity to be the result. And then others, like me at one point, build on dependability. To build on dependability means your completion as a person solely depends on your connection to someone else. This is such a dangerous place to be in for many reasons. Firstly, if you depend so much on a person being there, how do you function when they are not around? Secondly, too much expectancy in anyone results in unnecessary and constant disappointment. You should never give a person too much power over you. The more power a person holds in your life, the higher their ability of hurting you is. Don't get me wrong. It is nice having a support system. It is a beautiful thing to know that you have people you can count on when you can't rely on anyone else. Friendship is indeed a treasure, but it must never become an idol that imposes on your love for God or your love for yourself. Be extremely careful of the

> *THE STANDARDS THAT WE EXPECT OTHERS TO MEET MUST BE THE SAME STANDARDS THAT GOVERN OUR LIVES. IF NOT, WE ARE NOTHING MORE THAN HYPOCRITES SEARCHING FOR EVERYTHING WITHOUT GIVING ANYTHING.*

pedestal you place people on in your life. The main reason some of us tend to feel low in relationships is because we have placed people too high. At no point should loving anyone reduce who you are as an individual. Whenever you are loving someone but losing yourself in the process, you are wasting your time and your value. The truth is, most of the relationships we cling to, are not worth the pain we endure. Stop settling for anything just to be able to say that you have something. If mediocre is all that you accept, the better that you deserve won't ever show up at your door. It took for me to conclude, *"there has to be something better than this"* for me to actually go after better.

Make a vow to yourself that you will never spend another day being needy for human affection. Human affection can offer great joy but when you allow it to become a necessity, you will cry more than you smile; and you will grow further from God than you need to be. The only relationship that you will ever need is the one with God. In fact, for this very reason, God will disrupt any relationship that you have become too dependent on. I used to wonder why I would all of a sudden be disconnected from certain people and things. Eventually, I discovered: God will separate you from anything that separates you from Him. For some time, unexpected and unwanted interventions used to bother me until I understood that they were a demonstration of God's love for me. It is so humbling to know that God loves me enough to frustrate anything that stunts my fellowship with Him. His jealousy for me proves His pure love for me.

Who Are You Crying To?

My dependability on friendship made me develop a bad habit. I mean... a very bad habit. It's one of those habits that have become like second nature; I do it most times without even realizing it. After pondering, I knew I had to break this habit immediately; so with much determination, that's what I am working at. You are reading this waiting for me to stop beating around the bush, and to just go ahead and say what the bad habit is, right? I know you are. Well, you are waiting on me to say it and I'm waiting on you to guess it; can you? To the person whose guess is: an addiction to

Pepsi. You are so rightly wrong. Ha! While that is an addiction, and a very bad habit that I enjoy, that's not what I am referencing here, however. I am actually talking about the bad habit of calling for the wrong person first. Whenever I find myself in a crisis, I tend to reach out to a friend first. *Matters of the heart.* Even if it's something minuscule like me just having "one of those days", I'll find a friend to pour out my frustrations and feelings on. A bad habit! But also an expected habit because my dependability in people is entirely too high at times. Quite often, I can treat my friends as the 9-1-1 hotline, wanting them to be the first responders to every life event. Yes, being present in times of need comes with the duties of friendship, but the truth of life is, friends don't have all of the answers; they aren't always available; and some of them have too many broken things in their life to be a personal fixer to someone else. *We all know what happens when damaged people put too much time into fixing things for everyone but themselves, just ask Olivia Pope. Ooops, excuse me; I had a Scandal moment.*

> ℘
>
> *WHAT MAY BE A BURDEN TO OTHERS, GOD SEES AS AN OPPORTUNITY TO PROVE HIS LOVE FOR US BY COVERING OUR INSECURITIES AND WEAKNESSES UNDER THE BLANKET OF HIS GRACE.*
>
> ℘

After another reality check one day, I felt the push to stop this habit. I didn't know how I was going to do it but I just knew that I had to. My homeboy David's life inspired me to change the way I respond and whom I respond to. Whenever in distress, I have never known David to call his best friend or his mom. I'm sure they both were great people whom he could have depended on but he didn't use them as his 9-1-1 hotline. Instead, he would proceed directly to the Person he knew was more dependable and capable. All throughout the scriptures, my homeboy, David, would pick up the phone and dial Jesus' number before he would call anyone else.

Psalm 34:4 (NIV)
I sought the LORD, and he answered me; he delivered me from all my fears.

Psalm 118:5 (NIV)
When hard pressed, I cried to the LORD; he brought me into a spacious place.

Psalm 30:2 (NASB)
LORD my God, I called to you for help, and you healed me.

You see, these are only a very small percentage of the many scriptures that prove who David saw as the 9-1-1 representative of his life. David had a sure understanding that if He called out to God, God would not only listen to his petition for help but He would actually help him. God is not only a great listener; He's an outstanding deliverer as well. Another truth that can be learned from David's life and these scriptures is: God had David's heart. How can I conclude this? A clear indication of who has your heart is made evident by who you trust with your issues. Let me be absolutely clear. If you cry to your friends for help each and every time you are walking through the valleys of life, that is proof that your friends occupy a major space in your heart. Whoever has your heart will be the first to hear your cry.

In addition to Brother David, Apostle Paul also knew who to run to in times of hardship and weakness. In 2 Corinthians 12:8-9 (NIV), the Apostle pens: ***Three times I pleaded with the Lord to take it away from me. But he said to me, "My grace is sufficient for you, for my power is made perfect in weakness."*** You have to take these two nuggets from this passage:

1. **Know who can handle your thorn.** An unfortunate truth about relationships is: some people can only handle the aspects of you that are not flawed. Paul knew God wouldn't mishandle his weakness so that's why He consulted in Him.
2. **Don't misinterpret God's silence.** After not being answered the first time, He still went back to God. It's necessary that we become people that can continue praying when the only answer we

receive is no answer at all.

Very similar to Paul, a lot of us deal with some sort of weakness in at least one area of our life. There is a thorn piercing each of us. I will be the first to tell you, for every area that I'm seemingly successful in, I have another area that I struggle in. It's not because I'm a bad person; it's because I'm human. More now than ever before, I realize that our humanness is designed for the purpose of keeping our dependency in God's holiness. I've battled weakness and landed right at the brink of a nervous breakdown. Many nights, when it was just me and the reality of life, I remember wishing for a friend to pour my heart out to; but because I didn't know who could handle my humanness and not wanting to be a burden on anyone, I suffered in silence. Silly me! The hymnist said it best: *Oh, what peace we often forfeit. Oh, what needless pain we bear, all because we do not carry everything to God in prayer.* What may be a burden to others, God sees as an opportunity to prove His love for us by covering our insecurities and weaknesses under the blanket of His grace.

Grace Challenge

Friends are great but they don't hold the power to do the things that God can. Both David and Paul realized this. I'm sure they trusted and valued their friends, but they were still able to comprehend the difference between human abilities and divine assistance. We must be willing to do the same today. Whatever your thorn or insecurity may be, understand that God specializes in the matters of the heart. Today, I want you to stop for a moment of contemplation. Ask yourself: *Who holds my heart? When's the last time I cried out to God? Is my dependency more in people or in God?* At the end of the day, when it's all said and done, God will never leave us, nor forsake us. He will never violate our vulnerability by not answering us when we call Him. If God isn't the primary holder of your heart, make some adjustments today.

Chapter 6

Put Away Pretense

In this chapter, I want to speak to the heart that has been smiling, but can't remember the last time it felt joy; the person who has been laughing, but nothing is really funny; and to those of you who are breathing but barely living. Everyone sees you smiling, but no one knows that you dread going home at night because when you are alone, there is no escaping your disconcerting reality. Many people don't know that when you respond *"I'm doing okay"*, you need someone to look you in the eyes and realize that you are slowly losing a battle with depression. You want someone to read your inspirational Facebook status and realize that you are trying to encourage yourself by encouraging someone else, just to keep from breaking down.

Pretending is an art that has been mastered by the average person. In most cases, pretending is more about emotional defense than character deficiency. Let me explain. Fear is the initiator of certain behaviors. A lot of our actions (such as pretending) are because of what we don't want to happen to us and not because there is something wrong with us. People become guarded and use a mask of falsified strength as a shield from being let down and perceived as weak. A person who has suffered a series of letdowns in their past doesn't trust easily and the idea of vulnerability frightens them. Whenever someone is guarded and lacks emotionalism, it is usually for an understandable reason. We are often prone to judge those who are guarded and emotionally disconnected but we never take time to consider the experiences responsible for the wall that covers their hearts. Our experiences shape us into the people we are. The heart that you are attempting to love is probably one that has been battered by disappointment and bruised by neglect. There is a method to their madness, but you won't know it until you learn their history. Unless you make time to know (not judge) a person's past, you will never understand their present personality. In essence, if you meet a person who lives underneath a mask, chances are, they tried being their authentic self before and someone mishandled them; so now, they revert to pretense to remain protected.

It is true that everyone has their personal reasons as to why who they pretend to be in public doesn't reflect the shattered soul that stares back at them when they stand in the mirror. For the visionary, there are no conversations had about the issues in his personal life, because he is held to unfair standards that remove his right to be flawed. For the single lady, she accessorizes all of her outfits with independence because the last time she put faith in a man's presence and provision, he left her alone and destitute. For the teenage mom-to-be, she tells her mother that even though she is young, the pregnancy was planned because she knows she would be called a liar if she reveals that her uncle is the father of her unborn child; and her ears couldn't stand hearing that. For me, I showed up to church and work, and diligently tended to my responsibilities because as long as I was keeping busy, I could hide that I was internally bleeding.

> *OUR EXPERIENCES SHAPE US INTO THE PEOPLE WE ARE. THE HEART THAT YOU ARE ATTEMPTING TO LOVE IS PROBABLY ONE THAT HAS BEEN BATTERED BY DISAPPOINTMENT AND BRUISED BY NEGLECT.*

When Trust Is the Only Option

At a very young age, I got a sense of incredulity when it came to trusting people. On too many occasions, I was given promises that never became more than words; and it didn't help that the people who broke those promises were people that I loved and had immeasurable faith in. There is something about being let down by a loved one that penetrates your heart with a sting of disappointment, making you never want to hear another word from their mouth. The disappointments I faced over the course of my life eventually made me not want to look outside of myself for help regardless of how much I needed it. I made up my mind that if I was going to be weak, it wouldn't be with anyone else but me.

I had it so bad that there were many days I went hungry because I refused to ask someone for money or a meal. A major factor in this was pride. Although pride gave me a sense of comfort, I didn't know that pride isn't powerful enough to resolve trust issues and neither can it provide protection against disappointment. Even when I wanted to trust, pride was present, telling me not to and reminding me of all the times trusting went wrong. Pride has a tendency to make you believe that trusting can never work. So, I continued on not trusting. This behavior appeared advantageous for some time and then, BOOM, life happened and I hit rock bottom. There were many low moments in my life but none that were comparable to this one. I was at the lowest I had ever

A PROBLEM MAY NEVER BECOME SOLVED, BUT PRAYER REMINDS YOU THAT ALL THINGS WILL WORK TOGETHER FOR YOUR GOOD AND GIVES YOU THE POWER TO KEEP LIVING UNTIL THEY DO.

been. Once more, I was in the valley of life. The only difference this time was, I couldn't be my own hero and save myself. If I was going to make it out of this place, it was going to be because I found the strength to be weak enough to ask someone for help. It does not matter how long you live underneath a mask, your pretense will be challenged. The day will eventually come when every pretender has to conquer their trust issues and pull the veil off of their vulnerability.

What started as a good day quickly became an unexpected nightmare; and my ears had gotten news that my mind was not prepared to understand and my heart wasn't in a condition to accept. When they said, "life is full of swift transitions", they were not exaggerating in the least bit. Just as sure as my name is Khasmin, life had taken a quick turn down a road I didn't imagine myself traveling.

A few moments after the conversation had come to a conclusion, the feeling that I felt when I was removed from my home and placed into foster care, fell over me. Feeling like I just couldn't get life right and extremely tired of being dealt a bad hand, I sat in the bathroom and cried. Since that conversation, I have been a student in trust's classroom.

Completely flabbergasted and without any means to rectify this problem, I had to find the courage to confide in someone. There were people who I told, not because I expected them to help me solve the problem, but I trusted them enough to keep me covered in prayer while the problem was ongoing. When you are in between a rock and a hard place, you don't need problem solvers; you need prayer partners. You need someone who can stand in the gap on your behalf and intercede for you when you are too dispirited to pray for yourself. A problem may never become solved, but prayer reminds you that all things will work together for your good and gives you the power to keep living until they do.

As I was saying, I was officially homeless with only two options on the table: keep the situation to myself and suffer in silence or tell someone and admit that I needed help. Under normal circumstances, the first option would have won my vote, but there was a piece of me that wanted (and knew I had to) to give trust a try; and so I did.

Having to deal with this dilemma taught me some valuable lessons about life and faith:

1. It takes courage to admit that you are too weak to do life on your own.
2. Trusting might disappoint you, but it can never hurt you when you are protected by grace. Grace guards your heart in times of vulnerability.
3. By choosing not to trust, you can miss your biggest blessing. The person you are skeptical about trusting just might be more trustworthy than the ones you are most comfortable with trusting.
4. When you are in need, you shouldn't accept every favor offered. Most helping hands belong to gossiping mouths. If being in a position of need taught me nothing else, it certainly taught me that some

people only want one thing out of helping you—bragging rights. Whether it is buying you a meal, giving you a place to stay, or putting a few dollars into your bank account, there are individuals who do these things just so they will have something to add to their gossip bank.

Take the Chance

In life, there are going to be days when your strength alone is sufficient; and then there will be days when you are going to need a shoulder to lean on and ears to hear your cry. And that is quite alright. Give yourself permission to be weak, so that you don't break from the pressure of pretending to have it all together. You should never allow yourself to believe that being weak makes you inferior. Every strong person has weak moments. In fact, your greatest strength is developed through your deepest pains. Needing help does not make you less than; it only reaffirms that you are human. Instead of forcing yourself to do life on your own, learn how to depend on God and loyal people who understand your heart and have your back. Loyal people are rare but they do exist. If you find one person who will commit to being a faithful friend on a "no matter what" basis, you will never have to be alone.

In order to share a healthy relationship with a faithful friend, you can't mask your vulnerability; and you must be honest about your pain. I had grown so used to being a helping hand for everyone else that I did not know how to put my hand out for help when I needed it. I'm sure many of you reading this book share this same dilemma. You are the person that everyone calls when they are in need of support because they know that you will answer and show up. But the same way that you show up for others when they are in need, you will need others to

THE GRACE THAT YOU NEED CAN BE IN THE QUESTION YOU ARE TOO TIMID TO ASK; THE CONVERSATION YOU ARE AVOIDING; THE PERSON YOU ARE SCARED TO TAKE A CHANCE WITH.

show up for you when you are in need. You cannot live your whole life just being a giver. Yes, it is better to give than it is to receive; but if you are always giving and never receiving, what kind of life are you really living? Allow yourself to receive. Allow others to love you in return for the love you have given them. It is okay to be blessed even when it does not come from those that you have personally blessed.

You have to have enough faith in God to know that He has enough sovereignty to place tenderhearted people in your life who will make selfless deposits to get you from where you are to where you are destined to be. That is what He did for me. Some days He used my friends and family, other days He used perfect strangers.

Shaun, I thank you for being there. You have been the hero most friends never become; and not once did you make me regret being vulnerable with you. Thank you Taneka for being the support that reassured me grace does come with unfamiliar faces.

You make your own life miserable by attempting to live it on your own. Be open to the many positive possibilities trusting someone other than you has to offer. I know it is difficult to do when you are so used to being strong, but you have to learn how to trust someone other than yourself.

The grace that you need can be in the question you are too timid to ask; the conversation you are avoiding; the person you are scared to take a chance with.

In your trying times, don't just pray for help. After you have prayed, keep your eyes and mind open so you don't overlook your miracle. Too often our limited mindsets make us miss answered prayers. You may be expecting your help to come from within your circle of friends, but God may have plans to give you favor through someone you have only known for a short amount of time.

Grace is too big to be boxed in. It won't always show up in the form of a familiar face. Learn how to accept God's provision even when it doesn't match your personal expectation or preference. Accomplishing this may come with a challenge of conquering your pride. Pride doesn't only paralyze your ability to ask but it can also be the reason that you inadvertently reject the help you asked for.

When you finally take the chance at trusting, be okay with hearing no. You are going to hear no from people who genuinely cannot help you, and you are going to hear it from people who can but choose not to. Either way, each no will place you closer to the one yes that you need. Rejection can be good for you. It won't seem like it at the moment, but eventually the benefits of being told no will manifest; and once the sting of disappointment has faded away, you will appreciate that all things didn't work according to your plans.

In hindsight, I owe so much thanks to my Mama Benn (the lady who is a mother to me, and loves me as if she carried and birthed me) for telling me no when I was trying to hold on just to remain where I was comfortable being complacent. Earlier in the chapter, I told you that I was practically homeless because my current living arrangements were interrupted. My mama had the ability to bring resolution to the situation, but I am so grateful that she didn't. I can guarantee you that releasing me wasn't easy for her (because I'm her favorite son), but sometimes a part of loving someone is knowing when the time has come to let them go. It doesn't mean that you love them any less; it just means that you are wise enough to discern the change of time and seasons.

Being let go of is never easy to cope with, but you can find peace in knowing that it pushes you further into your purpose. It might feel as if they cut you off, but what if I told you that it needed to happen that way? What if God knew you were too blinded by love to walk away on your own so He made things too uncomfortable for you to stay? What pushes you out of your comfort zone pushes you into the direction of your destiny. Don't resist disconnections and learn not to take every goodbye personal. One day you are going to look back and thank God for loving you enough to disconnect you from people, places, and things.

<u>Grace Challenge</u>

If reading this chapter caused you to realize that your trust issues have transformed you into a person of pretense and a person that resists trusting others, I want to offer three practical steps that will help you remove the mask so that you can enjoy the fullness of life and not be someone breathing but barely living.

Step 1: Own that you have trust issues.

Step 2: Identify what the root causes of these trust issues are and then develop a plan to overcome them and be willing to devote yourself to that plan.

Step 3: Trust yourself enough to trust God and others.

Chapter 7

Give Yourself Grace

All throughout the book, I have mostly spoken about how life happened to me and my experiences with others throughout the years; but what I did not spend much time talking about are the many times I was responsible for penning pain in my own story. It is a hard pill to swallow, but the harsh truth is, sometimes it is our own behavior that pushes the pause button on our purpose.

Who wants to take the blame for being the creator of their own misery? Not I. At many times in my life, it was my mistakes and shortcomings that made my world chaotic. If you have ever failed yourself, you know exactly what I am talking about. There are few things harder than looking in the mirror and knowing that the person staring back at you is the one who has failed you, disappointed you, and held you back. That moment is more than a reality check; it is a slap in the face and a hurtful blow to your confidence and self-esteem. It presents you with the challenge of figuring out how to still love you even though you made a mistake and got it wrong somewhere along the journey.

One random day, I evaluated my life and began to think about where I was and where I thought I should have been but wasn't because of my own decisions and mistakes. I pondered the many things that I didn't accomplish, the hurdles I did not try to overcome, the friendships that were unworthy priorities that I gave my focus to, the many wrong investments, and so on and so forth. The more I thought about it, the more upset with myself I became. Before I knew it, that anger gradually became resentment; and let me just say this: *resentment becomes a completely different ballgame when the recipient of your resentment is you.* When you have resentment in your heart towards your own self, life becomes exceedingly complicated and it slowly reduces the belief that you have in yourself. The lack of belief has the potential to make life come to a complete standstill. Why? Anyone who doesn't have enough courage in themselves will not go after their purpose because regret makes you dwell on your shortcomings. That is what happened to me. For a long while, I didn't do anything that seemed beyond my ability to get right because my mind was still wrapped around what I had done wrong before.

> *"IF YOU DON'T ALLOW GOD TO HEAL YOU FROM THE MEMORY OF THE MISTAKE, YOU WILL BURY YOUR DESTINY IN THE VALLEY OF DRY BONES."*
> *IF YOUR MIND DOES NOT RECEIVE HEALING, YOUR HEART WON'T RELEASE THE REGRET THAT YOU ARE HOLDING.*
> *- SHAUN SAUNDERS*

There comes a time when you have to try again. My big brother, Shaun, said something so profound and it has stuck with me since I heard it. He said, and I quote, "If you don't allow God to heal you from the memory of the mistake, you will bury your destiny in the valley of dry bones." If your mind does not receive healing, your heart won't release the regret that you are holding. A regret filled heart is a heart that is incapable of loving anyone including the person who it belongs to. In order to rid your heart and life of regretful memories and indignant feelings toward yourself, you absolutely must aggressively deal with what is on the inside of your mind. In order to combat the negative thoughts that control your thinking and your view of yourself, you need to begin by adjusting your thinking from someone who failed to someone that is deserving of a second chance. Until you believe that you are worth being forgiven by yourself, you will never take the initiative to forgive yourself. Before that can happen, it is crucially important that your old way of thinking is done away with. The battle of overcoming regret with forgiveness begins and ends in your mind.

DECEPTIVE COMPENSATION

As discussed in the previous portion of this chapter, we understand that, when you are resentful and regretful towards yourself, you deprive yourself of love. Given this, I want to share something very interesting with you that I came to notice about being controlled by resentment and regret. I think it will help you understand the detriment of not forgiving yourself. The consequence of not forgiving yourself is deceptive compensation. Deceptive compensation is influenced by regret; and it is the action of making yourself pay for what you did wrong by withholding love from yourself and giving it to others. Regret deceives you into believing that the cost for shortcomings is rejecting yourself but supporting others.

To illustrate deceptive compensation, here is a personal example: during periods of beating myself up for mistakes made and missed opportunities, I would invest excessive time into loving and supporting others—specifically anyone that was succeeding at things I failed at in the past. One half of me did it because I have an intrinsic desire to do so; and another half of me did it only to feel better about myself. Does this behavior remind you of yourself? If it does, you, too, have been making compensations grounded in deception.

DECEPTIVE COMPENSATION IS INFLUENCED BY REGRET; AND IT IS THE ACTION OF MAKING YOURSELF PAY FOR WHAT YOU DID WRONG BY WITHHOLDING LOVE FROM YOURSELF AND GIVING IT TO OTHERS.

Deception ends when you have knowledge of the truth. If you want to put an end to making deceptive compensations, be honest and tell yourself the truth. The truth is simply this: you do not have to pay for anything you have done wrong in the past by overindulging yourself in everyone else's life and neglecting all of your dreams, aspirations, and goals in the process.

Romans 12:12 (NIV)
Do not conform to the pattern of this world, but be transformed by the renewing of your mind. Then you will be able to test and approve what God's will is--his good, pleasing and perfect will.

Ephesians 4:23 (NLT)
Instead, let the Spirit renew your thoughts and attitudes

∽

THE PRESENCE OF GRACE DOES NOT EXEMPT US FROM FAILURES, BUT IT DOES EMPOWER US TO NOT GIVE UP ON OURSELVES AFTER WE HAVE FAILED. GOD'S GRACE DIDN'T END AT YOUR LAST MISTAKE SO NEITHER SHOULD YOUR LOVE FOR YOURSELF.

∽

Your mind is the entryway through which regret and resentment come. If you are going to defeat them in order to forgive yourself, you must retract your steps and revisit the place where you stopped believing in your own self. There are times when going a few steps backwards is the only way moving forward will ever be possible. In order to attain total healing and forgiveness, this work will require your efforts, as well as help from God. Be bold enough to give God access to your mind so that every thought and attitude that prevents you from moving on can be uprooted and removed.

Giving up on yourself will always be comfortable, but it will never be a healthy solution. When you decide to live with regret, you are actually choosing to live your life without purpose and passion. You are deciding to bury your destiny. As long as you are regretful, you will quit before you begin, talk yourself out of what God is calling you to, and you will never discover the abundance life has to offer.

We are not here to live a life that represents perfection; we are here to live a life that embodies grace. The presence of grace does not exempt us from failures, but it does empower us to not give up on ourselves after we have failed. God's grace didn't end at your last mistake so neither should your love for yourself.

You lie to yourself by telling yourself that you are content, when the truth is, shame has made you comfortable with not continuing. As life passes you by, you find another excuse to justify why you have not progressed. Aren't you tired of forcing yourself to fit in where you don't belong? Aren't you tired of blaming previous mistakes and bad decisions for why your potential is not being maximized? If your answer is yes, do something about it.

Grace Challenge

Tell yourself that you are sorry. Don't subject yourself to the kind of suffering that can be avoided by three simple words, *"I forgive me."* Your mouth holds the grace that your heart needs. You might have to stand in front of the mirror everyday and repeat those words until you feel forgiven, but if that is what it takes, do it. You are worth whatever work it will take to give yourself a new beginning.

Chapter 8

It's About Everyone But You

It is one thing to recognize that you are encountering trials; but to really see why you are encountering those trials is another story. When you are able to understand the purpose of your pain, that understanding cultivates an appreciation for the good, the bad, and the ugly. Without appreciation, it is common for one to become resentful. The moment that I began appreciating my process, I stopped being angry at it because my understanding supplied peace that I didn't even know I needed. If you haven't already, you should start embracing your process. If you search with the intention to find, you will see the good that is hidden underneath the ashes. Our inability to pinpoint the value in what hurt us hinders a better us from emerging from our broken pieces. Pain doesn't become purposeful until you change your mind about what has hurt you.

It is God's will that we give thanks in all things. When you learn to be thankful, even for trials, you prove that you have faith in God's ability to deliver you from affliction. God responds to faith. If you ever want to get God's attention, put your faith on display. An actualization of relentless faith demands attention from God. I know this now, but I couldn't fathom it back then. Coming to grips with being appreciative for affliction was a hard pill to swallow because how does someone express gratitude for that which is hurting them? In the absence of appreciation, frustrated emotions exist. Frustration does two things: it picks at your mind and stymies your peace which ultimately makes moving forward difficult. If your current situation has you vexed, it is possibly because you haven't yet found out why you are going through the things that you are going through. Therefore, you can't appreciate it. So long as you don't comprehend what it is that you are facing, you will deem it pointless and unnecessary. For this very reason, prayer is essential. In prayer, God will share with you something that will let you know that what you are going through isn't a waste of your time. When God showed me a glimpse of the reason for my affliction, my mindset changed instantly. From then on, I began to endure hardship as a good soldier. Most days, being a good soldier will mean continuing in the fight when you are bruised the most and waving the flag is the only thing you want to do. But remember, it is about everyone but you.

For Your Good. For Their Benefit.

I am positive the majority of you reading this are familiar with the Bible verse that says *"all things work together for the good of them that love the Lord and are called according to His purpose"* Romans 8:28 *(KJV)*. Most of us know that passage better than we know our social security numbers. Ain't it the truth? You don't have to concur, I know I'm talking right.

AS YOU TRAVEL DESTINY'S COURSE, YOU ARE GOING TO FIND YOURSELF IN POSITIONS YOU NEVER IMAGINED; YOU WILL END UP MANY PLACES WITHOUT PRIOR PLANNING; AND YOU WILL CRY A LOT MORE THAN YOU PREFER; BUT UNLESS SOMETHING HURTS YOU, HOW CAN YOU HELP HEAL OTHERS?

I want to submit to you that, whenever you are called to live a life of God-given purpose, it won't be a walk in the park. As you travel destiny's course, you are going to find yourself in positions you never imagined; you will end up many places without prior planning; and you will cry a lot more than you prefer; but unless something hurts you, how can you help heal others? There are going to be those days when you not only question your purpose but also your God. Purpose comes with a price that can only be paid through suffering. Please note that I am not referencing just any manner of suffering; I am talking about selfless suffering. It is the kind of suffering that has nothing to do with you but everything to do with someone else. It is the kind of suffering that works for God's glory, your good, and someone else's benefit. Have you ever undergone this kind of suffering?

The greatest example of selfless suffering and sacrifice was shown on the cross on which Jesus Christ was beaten, bruised, and died. Jesus didn't die because He deserved to; He died because we were in dire need of salvific rescuing. His life became the saving grace that our souls needed so badly. That's the most praiseworthy example of sacrifice the world will ever know.

There is nothing we can ever do that will come close to what Jesus did, however, there will be some crosses that we will have to bear for someone else's benefit. None of us are trial exempt. I say this from a personal standpoint. Yes, what I have dealt with has contributed to my growth, but it has also empowered me to help others. God didn't just assign a heap of obstacles to my path because He had nothing better to do; He did it because He expected me to live as physical proof to others, that even in the midst of what is seemingly a hopeless situation, hope still exists.

Seated in the auditorium of your life are people waiting to witness a grace production that will revive their desire to try again; to love again; to trust again; and to believe that life still has meaning.

Grace didn't cover me so that I could hide my testimony after being delivered from my trials. Nothing about grace is ever one-sided. God grants us grace to help us help someone else. After you are healed, you should help heal someone else. Once you have transitioned from trial to triumph, your priority should be helping someone else to make the same transition. So many people go through various issues, storms, and seasons throughout life and when they make it out, they keep their stories to themselves. What good is an untold testimony?

Some people don't share their stories because they are ashamed of its contents. Some people don't share their stories out of fear that they will be judged. Others don't share their stories simply because they have not yet grasped the fact that, the main objective of their going through and coming out is so that they would be able to reach out and help someone else to discover the purpose of their pain.

An entire population of people benefited from Jesus dying on the cross. Similarly, there are beneficiaries associated with your pain as well. Seated in the auditorium of your life are people waiting to witness a grace production that will revive their desire to try again; to love again; to trust again; and to believe that life still has meaning. Don't be a silent survivor. Your voice holds the key to someone's new beginning. Each day you are silent, you stunt someone's freedom. With every test that we encounter in life, there is a testimony attached to it. With every testimony, there is also an assignment attached to it. The assignment is simply telling someone how we made it through. It is just that simple. Survivors must learn to take on the responsibility of helping to rescue wounded soldiers.

It Takes Transparency

Don't get me wrong. I understand the fear that is associated with broadcasting your testimony. Telling your testimony requires transparency. It requires bravery and confidence. And most times, it is not so much that we are afraid to tell our testimony, but rather that we are afraid of being transparent. The topic of transparency is a touchy one for most of us; but the reality is, you won't succeed at being transparent until you have mastered trust. Trust gives you the freedom to be transparent. Trusting may have wounded you before, but this time, grace will make it work. You have to trust yourself and you have to trust your God. Trust that you are strong enough to be vulnerable and trust that your story is worth sharing. Trust that God won't allow you to stand in shame after telling your story. In so doing, you give your vulnerability a chance to come outside of its shell, so that your story can be heard by the ear that needs healing for their soul.

Personally, I have never been the type to live my life as an open book. There is a lot about me that most people don't know. It has nothing to do with being ashamed of the details of my life; I'm just careful about what parts of me I share with people because I understand that some people can only deal with the truth when it is dressed up and pretty but not when it is naked and ugly; and I have grown up enough to be okay with that. You don't need everyone to understand you. If you live life as your true self, the opinions of those who misunderstand and misjudge you matters not.

When my mind reflects on the countless number of people who can benefit from the hope that my testimony can provide, that is the moment transparency becomes worth it. This doesn't mean that I go around giving people a front row seat to watch past and present scenes of my life; and I'm not suggesting that you should either. Transparency should have some limits. Be wise with the broadcasting of your truth. Always know how much to tell, who to tell it to, and when the moment is right for you to tell it.

If you are totally opposed to sharing your testimony—the most fragile part of your existence—I want to challenge you to consider a few things. Take a moment to think about the young man who is contemplating suicide because he feels no one can relate to him and everything he is dealing with. What if the only thing he needs to give life another chance is your testimony? In your mouth, are the words that can reignite the self-worth and esteem of that young girl that was molested by the only man she ever loved and trusted.

Your testimony may not be for everyone, but it is most definitely for someone. Imagine what the world would be like if everyone who escaped the darkness of their past would become a light to the world by sharing their stories. What if we acted in grace to speak to the bruised hearts that God has predestined to benefit from our pain?

<u>Grace Challenge</u>

Wear your scars on your sleeves. Tell your truth with love and let your life speak volumes of hope. Each time you break your silence and share your story without shame, you add value to your scars and worth to your wounds. What heart will you help heal today?